HAPPY BIRT

TO

....

WITH LOVE FROM

.

....

And Michelle

HAPPY BIRTHDAY—LOVE . . .

Complete Series

HAPPY BIRTHDAY

Love, Michelle

ON YOUR SPECIAL DAY

ENJOY THE WIT AND WISDOM OF

MICHELLE OBAMA

FIRST LADY

Edited by Jade Riley

CELEBRATION BOOKS

THIS IS A CELEBRATION BOOK

Published by Celebration Books 2023
Celebration Books is an imprint of Dean Street Press

Text & Design Copyright © 2023 Celebration Books

Cover by DSP

ISBN 978 1915393 68 5

www.deanstreetpress.co.uk

HAPPY BIRTHDAY—LOVE, MICHELLE

First Lady Michelle Obama is the embodiment of what hard work, strength of purpose and natural talent will achieve. Of course she and her husband, former President Barack Obama, are historically important as the first African Americans to reach the White House; but their achievements both domestic and international, plus a distinct lack of scandal during eight years in office add to what make them truly great. During her tenure, the First Lady highlighted the importance of good nutrition, family meal time and exercise to combat childhood obesity. She even planted an organic garden on the South Lawn of the White House. Beyond the borders of her own nation, Mrs. Obama has fought for women's equality and education in an effort to make every country stronger. Certainly being a graduate of both Princeton and Harvard law school makes her an excellent role model for young girls but it is her role as "Mom-in-chief" to her two daughters, Sasha and Malia, that gives her the most joy.

Strong family roots provided Michelle with a tenacity and confidence to overcome the disadvantages of growing up on Chicago's impoverished Southside. But she has always found her background to be her greatest strength. From her loving parents she gathered her lighthearted approach; knowing that fun and laughter help make these circumstances surmountable. Since leaving office, Mrs. Obama has now penned two best-selling books, starred in a documentary film and produced *Waffles + Mochi*; a puppet-style television show to get kids cooking and learning about foods of the world. She does all of this with spectacular style and her big warm-hearted smile. Michelle Obama is the mom, the teacher and the leader we all wish for.

On your birthday, be inspired by Michelle Obama: a woman who has wings to fly, a voice she knows how to use and a heart for everyone in the world.

Michelle Obama

When they go low, we go high.

I was not raised with wealth or resources or any social standing to speak of.

Choose people who lift you up.

We have an obligation to fight for the world as it should be.

If I can have any impact, I want women to feel good about themselves and have fun with fashion.

I've seen firsthand that being president doesn't change who you are. It *reveals* who you are.

For every door that's been opened to me, I've tried to open my door to others.

Every day, the people I meet inspire me . . . every day, they make me proud . . . every day they remind me how blessed we are to live in the greatest nation on earth.

Friendships between women, as any woman will tell you, are built of a thousand small kindnesses . . . swapped back and forth and forth and over again.

At fifty-four, I am still in progress, and I hope that I always will be.

Barack is swagalicous.

The lesson being
that in life you
control what
you can.

Failure is a feeling long
before it becomes
an actual result. It's
vulnerability that breeds
with self-doubt and
then is escalated, often
deliberately, by fear.

America is just downright mean.

I never cut class. I loved getting A's, I liked being smart. I liked being on time. I thought being smart is cooler than anything in the world.

My mother's love has always been a sustaining force for our family, and one of my greatest joys is seeing her integrity, her compassion, her intelligence reflected in my daughters.

I hate fund-raising. Haaaaate it. Hate, hate it.

We learned about dignity and decency—that how hard you work matters more than how much you make
. . . that helping others means more than just getting ahead yourself.

The White
House is like
a really nice
a really nice
prison.

Like so many American families, our families weren't asking for much. They didn't begrudge anyone else's success or care that others had much more than they did . . . in fact, they admired it.

Everyone on Earth,
they'd tell us, was
carrying around an
unseen history, and that
alone deserved some
tolerance.

Fashion is about so much more than just a pretty pair of pumps or the perfect hemline. For so many people across the country, it is a calling, it is a career, and it's a way they feed their families.

My husband will tell you one of the most frequent questions he gets from world leaders is, 'How's your wife's garden?'

I view myself as being the average woman. While I am first lady, I wasn't first lady my whole life. I'm a product of pop culture. I'm a consumer of pop culture, and I know what resonates with people.

If proud Americans can be who they are and boldly stand at the altar with who they love then surely, surely we can give everyone in this country a fair chance at that great American Dream.

Education is
the single-most
important civil rights
issue that we face
today.

If my future were
determined just by my
performance on
a standardized test,
I wouldn't be here. I
guarantee you that.

I wake up
every day in a
house built by
slaves.

We needed now to
be resolute, to keep
our feet pointed
in the direction of
progress.

I am so tired of fear. And I don't want my girls to live in a country, in a world, based on fear.

I know what it feels like to struggle to get the education that you need.

With every word we utter, with every action we take, we know our kids are watching us. We as parents are their most important role models.

Elections aren't just about who votes but who doesn't vote.

What I have never been afraid of is to be a little silly, and you can engage people that way. My view is, first you get them to laugh, then you get them to listen.

Success is only meaningful and enjoyable if it feels like your own.

Time, as far as
my father was
concerned, was
a gift you gave to
other people.

You've got to vote, vote, vote, vote. That's it; that's the way we move forward. That's how we make progress for ourselves and for our country.

Here in America, we
don't give in to our
fears. We don't build
up walls to keep
people out.

I want kids to know:
Don't wait for somebody
to come along and
tell you you're special.
Because that may never
happen.

You see, at the end of the day, my most important title is still 'mom-in-chief.' My daughters are still the heart of my heart and the center of my world.

We learned about gratitude and humility – that so many people had a hand in our success, from the teachers who inspired us to the janitors who kept our school clean . . . and we were taught to value everyone's contribution and treat everyone with respect.

Do not die in the history of your past hurts and past experiences, but live in the now and future of your destiny.

No country can ever truly flourish if it stifles the potential of its women and deprives itself of the contributions of half of its citizens.

One of the lessons that I grew up with was to always stay true to yourself and never let what somebody else says distract you from your goals.

Women and girls can
do whatever they
want. There is no limit
to what we as women
can accomplish.

Don't let anyone speak for you, and don't rely on others to fight for you.

Being a healthy woman isn't about getting on a scale or measuring your waistline. We need to start focusing on what matters—on how we feel, and how we feel about ourselves.

To be a good parent,
you need to take care of
yourself so that you can
have the physical and
emotional energy to take
care of your family.

The childhood obesity issue is critically important to me because it's critically important to the health and success of our kids, and of this nation, ultimately.

Wounded Warriors tell me they're not just going to walk again, they're going to run, and they're going to run marathons!

The arts can enrich all of us in this nation as individuals. The arts can enrich all of our communities and the country. And the arts can connect us to each other like nothing else can.

I am an example of what is possible when girls from the very beginning of their lives are loved and nurtured by people around them. I was surrounded by extraordinary women in my life who taught me about quiet strength and dignity.

My happiness isn't connected to my husband's or my boss's or my children's behavior. You have control over your own actions, your own well-being.

"

Now I think it's one of the most useless questions an adult can ask a child—What do you want to be when you grow up? As if growing up is finite. As if at some point you become something and that's the end.

For me exercise is more than just physical, it's therapeutic.

Doing the impossible is the history of this nation. It is how this country was built.

Learning through the arts reinforces critical academic skills in reading, language arts and math and provides students with the skills to creatively solve problems.

Communities and countries and ultimately the world are only as strong as the health of their women.

Strong men—men who are truly role models—don't need to put down women to make themselves feel powerful. People who are truly strong lift others up. People who are truly powerful bring others together.

Every girl, no matter
where she lives,
deserves the opportunity
to develop the promise
inside of her.

We should always have three friends in our lives—one who walks ahead who we look up to and follow; one who walks beside us, who is with us every step of our journey; and then, one who we reach back for and bring along after we've cleared the way.

You can't make decisions based on fear and the possibility of what might happen.

We need to do a better job of putting ourselves higher on our own 'to do' list.

As women, we must stand up for ourselves. We must stand up for each other. We must stand up for justice for all.

Don't fear your dreams, thoughts, or ideas. Live life fully and help those around you.

Be passionate about something and lean to that strength.

My job, I realized,
was to be myself,
to speak as myself.
And so I did.

You've got to make choices that make sense for you because there's always going to be somebody who'll think you should do something differently.

If you don't get out there and define yourself, you'll be quickly and inaccurately defined by others.

Bullies were
scared people
hiding inside
scary people.

My kids are normal. If they could eat burgers and fries and ice cream every day, they would. And so would I. But that doesn't sustain us.

We need an
adult in the
White House.

Here in America, we don't let our differences tear us apart . . . No, we're all in this together. We always have been.

Dominance, even the threat of it, is a form of dehumanization. It's the ugliest kind of power.

I will not run for president. No, nope, not going to do it.

I want kids to know: Don't wait for somebody to come along and tell you you're special. Because that may never happen.

No one, I realized, was going to look out for me unless I pushed for it.

Your story is
what you have,
what you will
always have. It is
something to own.

You don't have to be somebody different to be important. You're important in your own right.

There is no magic to achievement. It's really about hard work, choices, and persistence.

Grief and resilience live together.

No matter who you are, no matter where you come from, you are beautiful.

Hope and change are hard-fought things.

We were planting
seeds of change,
the fruit of which we
might never see. We
had to be patient.

In my blinding drive to excel, in my need to do things perfectly, I'd missed the signs and taken the wrong road.

The journey doesn't end.

Michelle Obama

ABOUT THE EDITOR

JADE Riley is a writer whose interests include old movies, art history, vintage fashion and books, books, books.

Her dream is to move to London, to write like Virginia Woolf, and to meet a man like Mr. Darcy, who owns a vacation home in Greece.

Made in the USA
Thornton, CO
01/23/23 14:22:29

0c47cab1-3f4d-4fc0-b7d3-0ee4d982ec1cR02